Foreword

It is with great pleasure and honor that I write the foreword for the "Guide For Badminton - Homework & Warm Up". Great "Thanks" goes out to Syam, Eric and Zak for sharing their knowledge into a guide for anyone, young and old, to take up the sport of badminton for fun, exercise, and the pursuit of good health.

Who would have ever thought that playing badminton could connect one to an estimated 220 million players throughout the world! We truly enjoy this sport that transcends languages, cultures, and politics.

I hope your guide will pave the way for many more to enjoy the sport of badminton.

Kenneth Wong
Chairman of the Board
USA Badminton
US Olympic and Para Olympic Committee

Preface

Welcome to this short handy guide to improve your badminton skills, irrespective of whether you are a beginner, or an advanced player. The idea for this book was born when we were discussing ways to improve the skills of our students who took one-or-two classes weekly at Smashville, a club Eric founded in Pennsylvania, US. As the Founder of Durabird, a startup bringing patented durable natural feather shuttlecocks to the players, I was interested in establishing a Durabird- Smashville training program with Zak's help. When we searched for simple guides that we can recommend to our students as a handy reference, we found there were none.

In this guide, we put together our combined experience from club play, tournament play, and coaching, as well as tips given by some of the best national coaches. We hope you find this guide useful and use it responsibly. Best wishes for improving your badminton skills, as well as core strength needed to improve your game.

We thank Piyush Prakash for the illustrations' support for this book.

Syam, Eric, and Zak

Contents

Introductions

As one of many badminton builders and promoters of the sport in the USA, Badminton Goes Viral.org is proud to be associated and supportive of the efforts of the Durabird-Smashville Badminton Training Program.

Badminton is truly a lifetime sport for all and with health and fitness as the goal; the broad appeal of badminton is a fun way to achieve and maintain wellness. The "Homework and Warm Up" exercises provided in this book are valuable tools for both the recreational and competitive player to build strength and skills to become a better player and to stay at the top of their game.

We congratulate Syam, Eric and Zak on this fantastic contribution to the sport of badminton!

Paul Knechtel & Lisa J. Ward
Founders of Badminton Goes Viral
Co-Founders of Badminton NC
(The first dedicated badminton facility in North Carolina.; now part of Triangle
Badminton & Table Tennis)

Congratulations to the authors for their time and effort to develop Badminton sport across USA. The "Guide for Badminton Homework & Warm Up" covers an overall training schedule for Badminton Players that is narrated and presented in such a way that it could drive any commoner to start Badminton sport after reading the book. This will definitely help the current players to build up their training ability with right grip technique to sharpen their skills.

The book has also covered warm up and cool down exercises that is really good for the Badminton fraternity to play the game without injuries.

I wish you and your team to succeed in your efforts for promoting the sport.

Dr. Yuva Dayalan, PhD
Badminton Yoga Therapist
Director, Dayal Group
5 Guinness World Record Holder
Yoga Therapist & Trainer of Indian Badminton Team

Warning

This guide should be used in consultation with, or under the guidance of, a badminton coach as the repetitive movements, strenuous exertion, stretching, and other elements described here can cause physical injury to yourself, or others, and/or destruction of objects in your surroundings.

Make sure that enough space is available around you, and above your head, and you maintain a safe distance from other people, including children, before attempting any of the exercises described here.

The authors of the book assume no responsibility for bodily harm/injury, or destruction of property resulting from practicing the exercises described in this handbook.

Grip Strength and Flexibility

Forehand

- Note hand and finger placement with respect to the bat (front, side, etc.)
- The finger placements are different for forehand and backhand grips
- Practice fast transitions from position 1 to position 2
- Should hear the racquet whipping during each fast slapping/snapping transition
- Repeat 20 or more times for both forehand and backhand

The fingers move from relaxed to tight. The fingers will also rotate the racquet (typically right to left, clockwise, for a right hander) along with wrist.

Stand with the racquet perpendicular to the ground, and fingers relaxed; then tighten the fingers on the racquet to "slap" the racquet forward using only your fingers.

You could practice the same without a racquet, this time with a motion holding the palm up and slightly to the right of your face facing toward you and then pronating (turning) the palm up and out so it ends up facing away from you.

Position 1 **Position 2**

One view

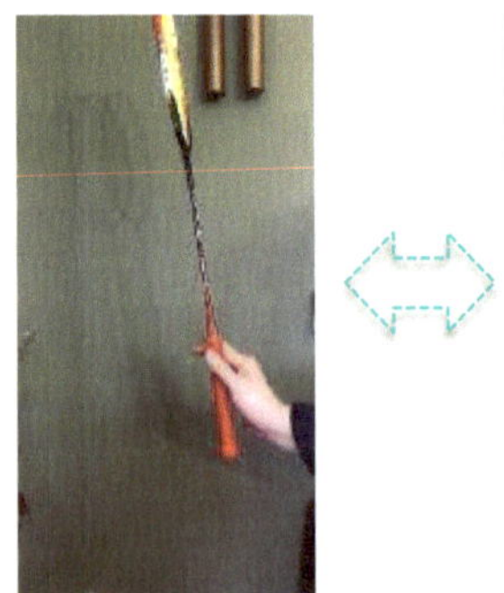 

A different view

Grip Strength and Flexibility

Backhand

- Note hand and finger placement with respect to the bat (front, side, etc.)
- They are different for forehand and backhand grips
- Practice fast transitions from position 1 to position 2
- Should hear the racquet whipping during each fast slapping/snapping transition
- Repeat 20 or more times for both forehand and backhand.

As in forehand, the fingers move from relaxed to tight.

Stand with the racquet perpendicular to the ground, and fingers relaxed; then tighten the fingers on the racquet to "slap" the racquet forward using only your fingers.

You could   practice the   same   without   a racquet.

Unlike forehand, the hand won't turn/pronate during backhand.

Position 1

Position 2

Strength training for wrists

Wrist curl ups
Use 2-or-3-pound dumbbells
Rest hand on the edge of a flat surface
Curl wrists up, and then down
Do sets of 20
Reverse/turn wrist and repeat

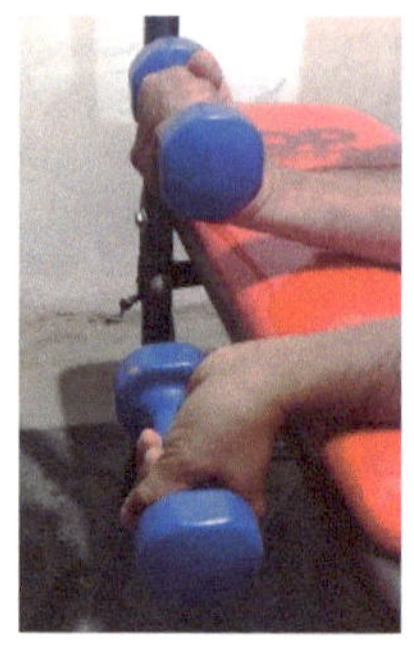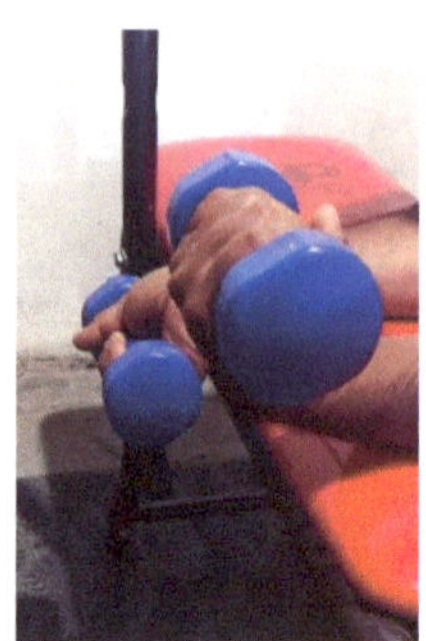

repeat, focusing on the racquet hand

Wrist roller
Tie a small weight to a short rod using a string or rope and rest the weight on the floor
Stretch hands out as shown
Roll the weight up and then down
Do 5 sets
Reverse your hold (palms up versus palms down) and

Strength training for fingers

Use an adjustable hand gripper such as the one shown
Adjust tension to not-too- easy/not-too-tough
Do sets of 20 for index- middle
Do sets of 20 for middle- pinky
Do sets of 20 for thumb

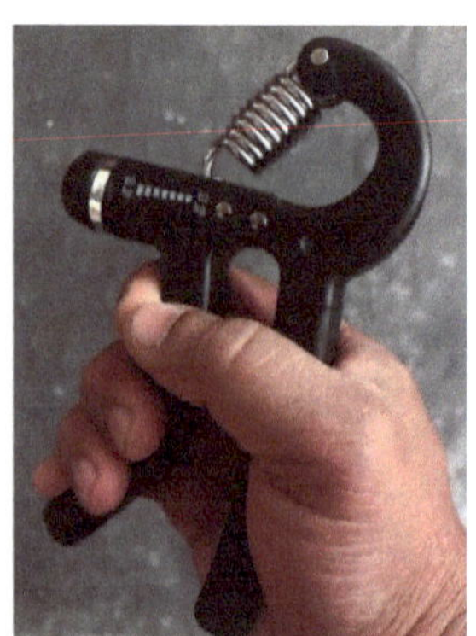

Strength training for arms

Pushups on parallel bars (hanging rings or floor)
Start with 5, and slowly increase to 20.

Pull-ups on parallel bars (or hanging rings)
Start with 5, and slowly increase to 20.

Strength training for legs

1 JUMPING JACKS
Start with 20, and increase to 100

2 SQUATS
Start with 20, and increase to 100

3 SINGLE LEG SQUATS (FRONT)
Start with 2, and increase to 10

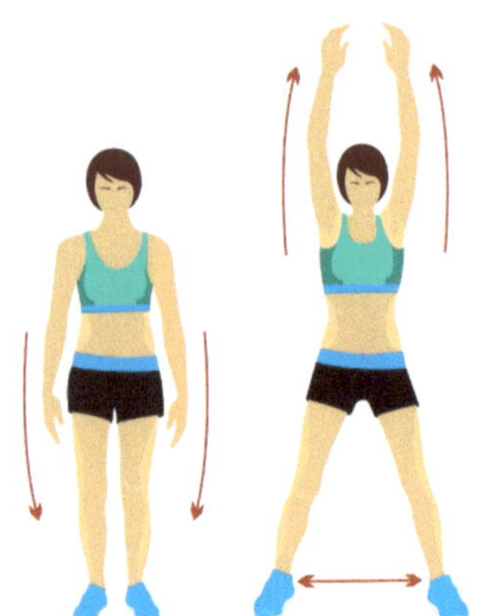

4 STEPS
Start with 50, and increase to 200

5 SINGLE LEG SQUATS (SIDE)
Start with 2, and increase to 10

6 ROPE JUMP

Start with 30 seconds jumping, and 15 seconds break three times.
Increase by 15 seconds every two weeks up to 3 minutes

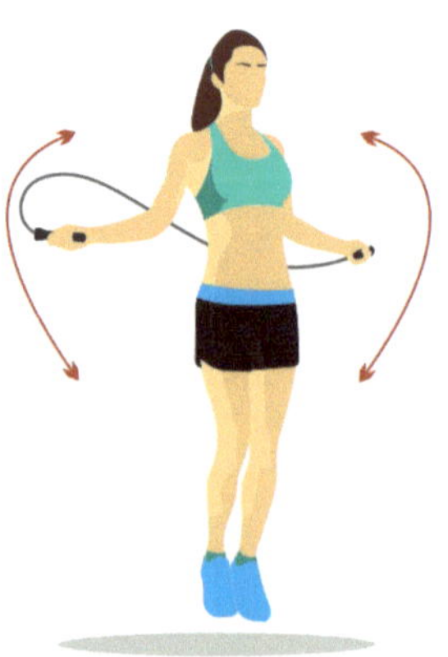

Cardio

These are guidelines to increase your stamina.

How far you can take this depends on your level of fitness.

Recommended minimum is two times a week.

First month
Run half mile-long distance. 2X100 meter sprints after the long distance.

Second month
Run ¾ mile long distance. 1X200 meter sprint after the long distance.

Third month
Run one-mile long distance. 2X100 meter sprints after the long distance.

Fourth month onwards
Add ¼ of a mile to the long distance run every month. Alternate between 1X200 and 2X100 meter sprints **after** the long distance.

Year-end goal
By the end of the first year, your goal must be to run 3 miles long distance two times a week, along with the sprints

Serve/Service

This serving practice exercise may be practiced indoors or outdoors. It may also be set up in a home recreation room, garage, or basement.

Place a piece of tape on the wall 5 ft. high.

Stand back 6 ft.

Rotate left face of racquet toward you and place in front of stomach with elbow up (for right-handers).

Hold a birdie/shuttlecock several inches in front of the strings, on the outer face of the racquet.

Try to serve as close as possible to, but above the tape on the wall, by hitting the bottom of the shuttlecock with the racquet.

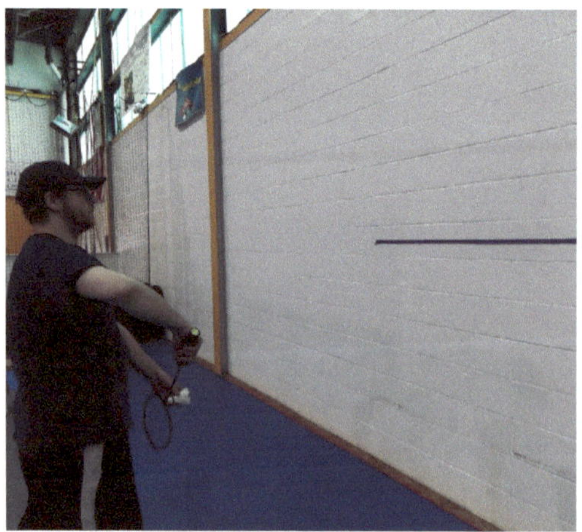

Reflex

Stand back 5 feet from a wall.

Hit the shuttlecock against the wall around 5 feet high (net height).

When the shuttlecock returns, hit it again against the wall, repeating until you miss. Aim, and try to hit the same spot around net height.

In the first couple of months, aim for 50-100 repeated hits before a miss, constantly trying to improve your record of non-stop hits as you progress.

Shadow exercise: Net kills

Practice shadow exercises with a racquet or a grip device as shown in the picture*
below

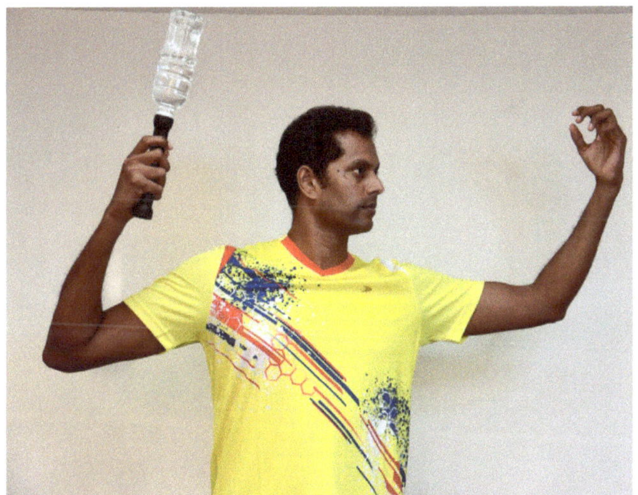

Net kills

Imagine the shuttlecock at different heights as shown below. Now, imagine your elbow at the center of a circle. Neutral position is the starting position of the racquet on the circumference/edge of the circle. Grey areas on the circle show how much the wrist/arm moves back and forth during each kill. Tighter the shuttle is to the net, tighter the forearm-wrist action.

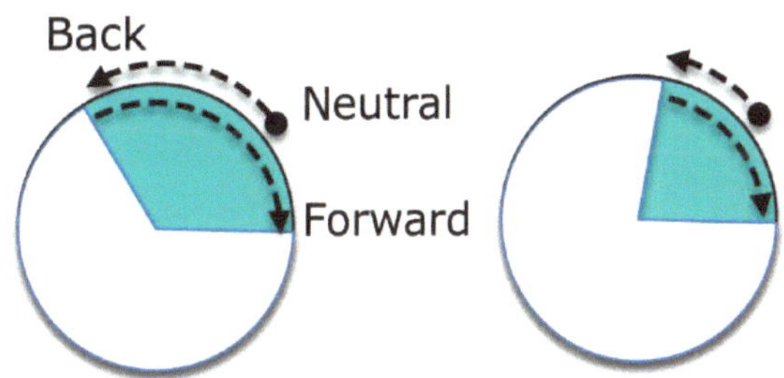

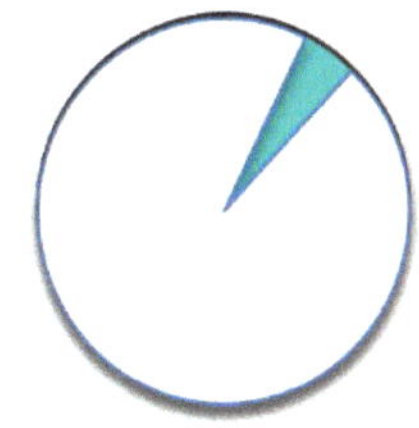

Shuttle well above head
Smash with wrist

Shuttle around head
Drive with wrist

Shuttle below head
Tap with wrist

Shuttle tight on net
Slice sideways with wrist

*The pictures of the grip device shown in picture was reproduced with permission from Dayal sports

Shadow exercise:
Smash-defense forehand, backhand

Imagine the shuttlecock above your head. Now, imagine your elbow at the center of a circle. Neutral position is the starting position of the racquet on the circumference/edge of the circle. Grey areas on the circle show how much the wrist/arm moves back and forth during each action

Clear

Do 5 sets of 10 on forehand
Repeat on backhand

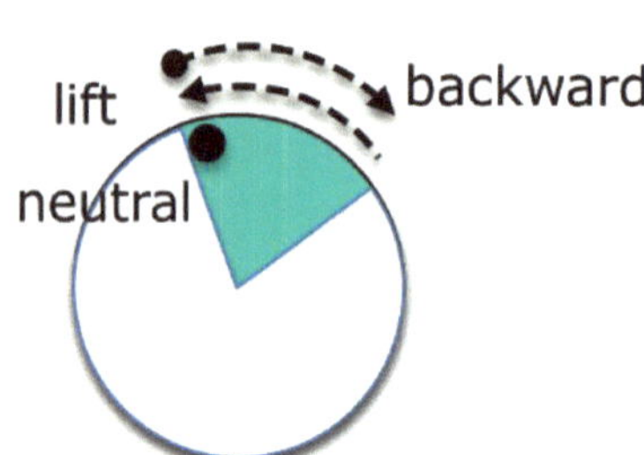

Drive

Do 5 sets of 10 on forehand
Repeat on backhand

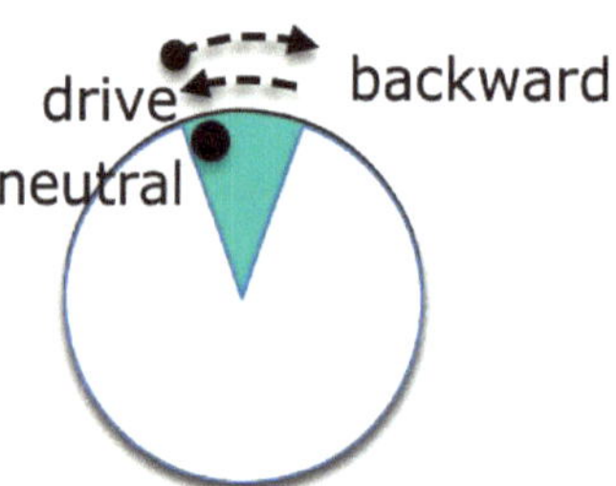

Drop

Do 5 sets of 10 on forehand
Repeat on backhand

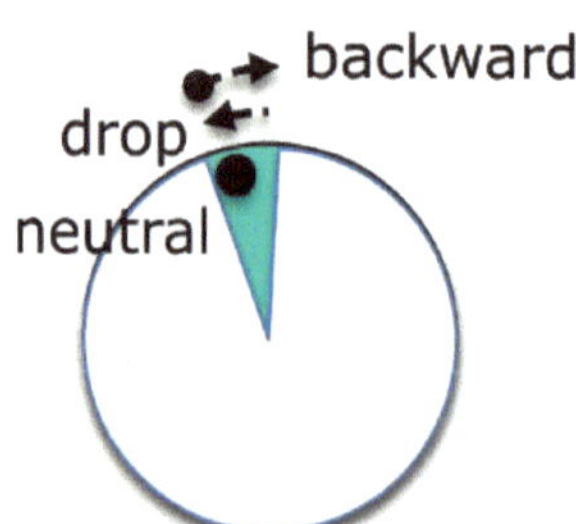

Shadow exercise: Wrist-Hand Power Training

Imagine the shuttlecock above your head. Now, imagine your elbow at the center of a circle. Neutral position is the starting position of the racquet on the circumference/edge of the circle. Grey areas on the circle show how much the wrist/arm moves back and forth during each action.

Backhand drive
Do 5 sets of 10

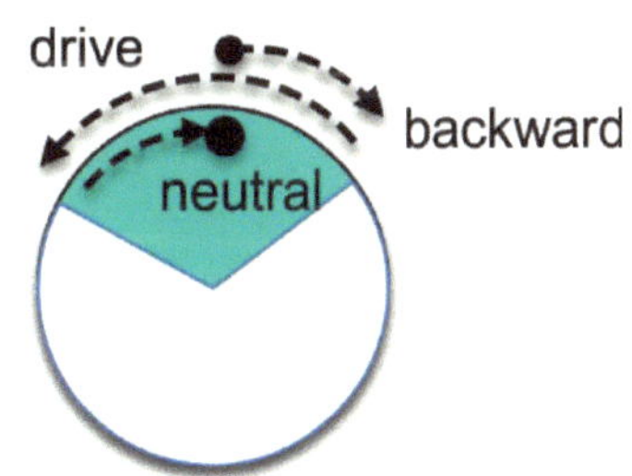

Forehand smash
Do 5 sets of 10

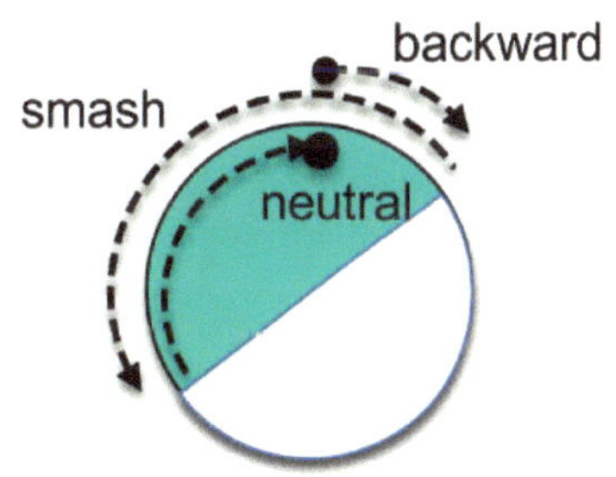

Backhand clear
Do 5 sets of 10

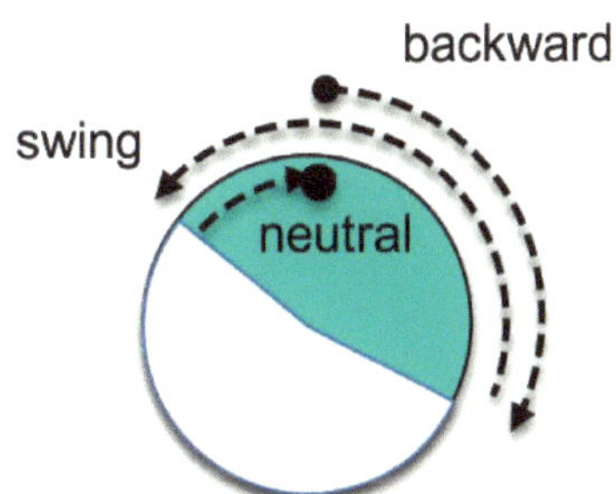

Strength training for back

Repeat each exercise for the number of times shown against each one

Strength training for abs

Repeat each exercise for the number of times shown against each one

Stretching routine for warming up before play
Full routine (continued on next page)
Repeat each one a minimum of five times without rushing through
Also, do the routine for both sides of the body

Stretching routine for warming up before play
Full routine

Repeat each one, a minimum of five times without rushing through
Also, do the routine for both sides of the body

Stretching routine for warming up
Minimal routine- waist

Keep your feet apart as shown.

Turn your body from one side to the other as shown with your hands stretched outward and relaxed.

Repeat 20 times.

Stretching routine for warming up
Minimal routine- back

Keep your feet crossed as shown-one foot in front of the other.

Bend/stretch your body and touch your toes with your fingers and stay in position for 10 seconds.

Switch legs so that the foot that was in front is now behind the other foot.

After switching the legs, repeat stretching by touching the toes again with your fingers. Repeat 20 times.

Stretching routine for warming up
Minimal routine- wrist and ankles

Hold palms together with the fingers locked as shown.

Keep one leg stretched behind as shown.

Rotate the wrist 20 times in one direction.

At the same time, rotate the ankle of the
leg stretched back 20 times.

Switch to the other leg by stretching it back and rotating it.

Change the direction of rotating the wrists when
you switch your leg.

Try to make the rotations smooth and less jerky.

Repeat rotating the wrist and leg 20 times.

The End

LOVE BADMINTON
Offense
Shots
Smashes
Netkills
Serves
Forehand
Lift
Stance
&
Grip
Bounce
Backhand
Footwork
Drives
Drops
Blocks
Defense
© Durabird 2019 www.durabird.com